ORCAS

by Beth Adelman

Stride
An Imprint of The Child's World®
childsworld.com

The Child's World
childsworld.com

Published by The Child's World®
800-599-READ • www.childsworld.com

Photography Credits
Cover, 1: Wirestock/Dreamstime.com
Interior: AP Photos: Don Ryan 26; John McConnico 27. Dreamstime.com: Mickem 23B; Meunierd 25T. Ian Froud: 25B. Shutterstock: Tory Kallman 2, 16, 17, 18; Wirestock 5; Buchpetzer 6; Slowmotiongli 7; Tatiana Ivkovich 8; Coulanges 9; Monika Wieland Shields 10; Wildestanimal 11, 19; Karoline Cullen 12; Willyam Bradbury 14T; Foto 4440 14B; BlueRingMedia 15; Nick Grobler 20; 2009fotofriends 21; Jiri Kulisek 22; JKerrigan 23T, 31; Pixhound 24; Maria Harvey 28; Bborris67 29.

ISBN Information
9781503858169 (Reinforced Library Binding)
9781503860742 (Portable Document Format)
9781503862104 (Online Multi-user eBook)
9781503863460 (Electronic Publication)

LCCN 2021952454

Printed in the United States of America

BRINGING THE WORLD TO YOUNG READERS 1968

TABLE OF CONTENTS

CHAPTER 1

ORCA BASICS

You think sharks are the baddest creatures in the ocean? Think again! Orcas are the ocean's super **predators**. They're **mammals**, the largest, fastest members of the dolphin family. They're strong, smart, and deadly.

They're big, too. Male orcas can be 28 feet (9 m) long and weigh 12,000 pounds (5,443 kg). The females are only a little smaller—25 feet (8 m) long and up to 8,000 pounds (3,629 kg). Like all dolphins, orcas have torpedo-shaped bodies that glide smoothly through the water. When these powerful creatures chase a meal, they can go up to 45 miles (72 km) an hour!

Orcas used to be called killer whales. Now people understand that name is not correct. *Orca* comes from a Latin word that means "whale." The scientific name for the orca, *Orcinus orca*, is based on this Latin word.

Orcas are powerful enough to leap out of the water.

The icy-cold waters of the Arctic are no problem for thick-skinned orcas.

Orcas are found in almost all of the world's oceans. They usually stay in areas where the water is colder. They are often seen in the Arctic and Antarctic and around Alaska. Orcas also live off the coasts of northwest Canada, northern California, northern Europe, and Greenland.

Even from the shore, people can watch wild orcas doing what they do best—hunting.

An orca shows off its sharp teeth and powerful jaws.

Orcas eat fish, squid, and penguins. They also eat mammals such as seals, sea lions, and dolphins.

To help them eat, orcas have about 45 cone-shaped teeth. Each is about three inches (7.6 cm) long and is shaped for ripping and tearing **prey**.

This orca has just snagged a small seal amid a huge splash of ocean water.

Like all great hunters, orcas see and hear very well. Their eyesight is good above and under the water, and they can hear a wide range of sounds. Their skin is very sensitive to touch, too.

HEARING ECHOES

Bats are another animal that uses echolocation. They often hunt at night in low light. They make clicking sounds that bounce off insects, which they hunt. The sounds also help the bats navigate through caves and forests in the dark.

Orcas use **echolocation** to find their way and to locate prey underwater. They make sounds like clicks. The sounds bounce off objects, and the echoes return to the orca's special hearing **organ**. Based on how quickly the sound returns, the animal can tell what is in front of it and where it is.

Orcas are mammals and give birth to live, air-breathing babies called calves. Calves are big babies! Newborn orcas are about 8 feet (2 m) long and weigh 300 to 400 pounds (136 kg to 181 kg)! The calves swim to the surface to breathe.

The calves drink their mother's milk for about a year and a half. Young orcas often stay with their mothers for 10 years or more. Living in a group helps young orcas learn their fearsome hunting skills.

A mother orca helps the smaller calf learn to rise to the surface to breathe.

Orcas usually swim near the surface so they can get air. But some can make dives lasting as long as 15 minutes.

How can you tell males from females? Look at the **dorsal** fin—the fin that sticks up on the whale's back. Often, males have a very tall dorsal fin shaped like a triangle. It can be six feet (2 m) tall. Most females' dorsal fins are only about three feet (1 m) tall and are curved.

CHAPTER 2

AN ORCA'S LIFE

Orcas live in groups called **pods**. There are usually about five to 30 animals in a pod. "Superpods" of 100 orcas have also been spotted. A pod is like a family, and some pods stay together for many years.

Orca pods are made up of many smaller family groups.

Pods do everything together, including traveling and hunting. Sounds make it easier for pod members to live and work together. Orcas use whistles, buzzing sounds, and screeches. Each pod has its own style of calls. This language helps the members feel like a family.

Scientists who study orcas in the wild can tell which pod is nearby just by listening to the calls the whales make.

A group of orcas surfaces together. Working together, orcas can "chase" a school of fish.

Orcas are such successful hunters because all the animals in the pod work together. For example, pod members sometimes force lots of fish into one area and then take turns feeding. In other cases, the members join forces to surround a larger animal, such as a blue whale. They wear the animal down until it becomes a meal.

Orcas have other ways of catching their prey. Sometimes they smack into the edge of a small piece of floating ice.

This daring orca has splashed onto a beach while trying to grab seals resting there.

The sudden blow can knock a resting seal into the sea! Some orcas will actually slide up out of the water and onto a beach to grab an animal. Orcas have been seen attacking seals on a beach. The orca charges up through shallow water to try to snatch a seal from the sand.

ARCTIC OCEAN FOOD CHAIN

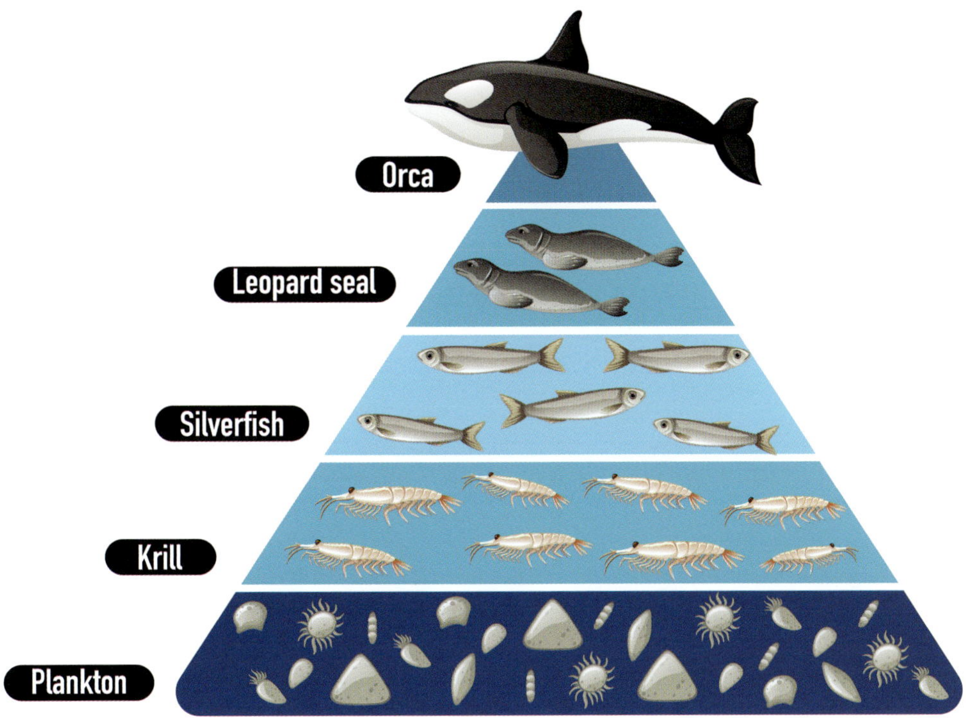

Ocean mammals and big fish eat smaller fish. Those fish eat even smaller fish, who eat even tinier creatures. This list of animals that eat other animals is called a food chain. Orcas are on the top of the Arctic food chain.

Up, up, and away. An orca can leap so that its whole body leaves the water.

Orcas are also awesome **acrobats**. Big adults often "breach," throwing themselves up out of the water in splashing body twists. When they're "spyhopping," they pop their heads and upper bodies up from the waves and swim backwards. They also slap their tail fins or dorsal fins on the water, making a loud sound.

Scientists think these acrobatics are the animals' ways of expressing their feelings. They might be showing feelings of excitement or anger. They might even be inviting others to play. Scientists think spyhopping might be a way of looking around, since orcas often do this when boats get close.

When spyhopping, the whales' eyes come above the surface.

Using sounds, orca pods move in the same direction.

People in different families, communities, and countries often have different ways of behaving. Orca pods in different areas have different ways of behaving, too.

Some orcas live in large groups. Others travel in smaller groups, and members of the group come and go. Others live far out at sea, and scientists don't know much about those groups. The different kinds of orca groups have their own ways of hunting and communicating, and places they like to go.

One important part of being in a pod is working together. Teamwork often helps gather food. For example, near Norway, orcas herd schools of herring into tight balls of fish. After **stunning** the herring with smacks of their tails, the orcas swoop in to eat them.

While holding its breath, the orca uses its powerful tail to move under the water.

These differences aren't just about eating, either. In the Crozet Islands, between Antarctica and South Africa, the orcas visit **kelp** beds. Several times a day, they swim through the long, thick strands of seaweed. They don't eat anything while they're in the kelp beds. They just seem to like the feeling of swimming through them.

Swimming in grass? This orca cruises through a shallow bed of kelp.

There are kelp beds off the coast of northern California, too. But the orcas who live there don't swim in them at all.

Orcas in British Columbia, Canada, like to rub themselves on shallow, pebbly beaches. Other orcas who live near beaches don't do this.

Some orcas roll around on beaches with smooth rocks.

CHAPTER 3

ORCA STORIES

People all over the world have told tales about the awesome power of orcas. To some groups of people, the orca is a helpful animal. To others, it is a fierce predator. In the Pacific Northwest, orcas are important to many groups of people.

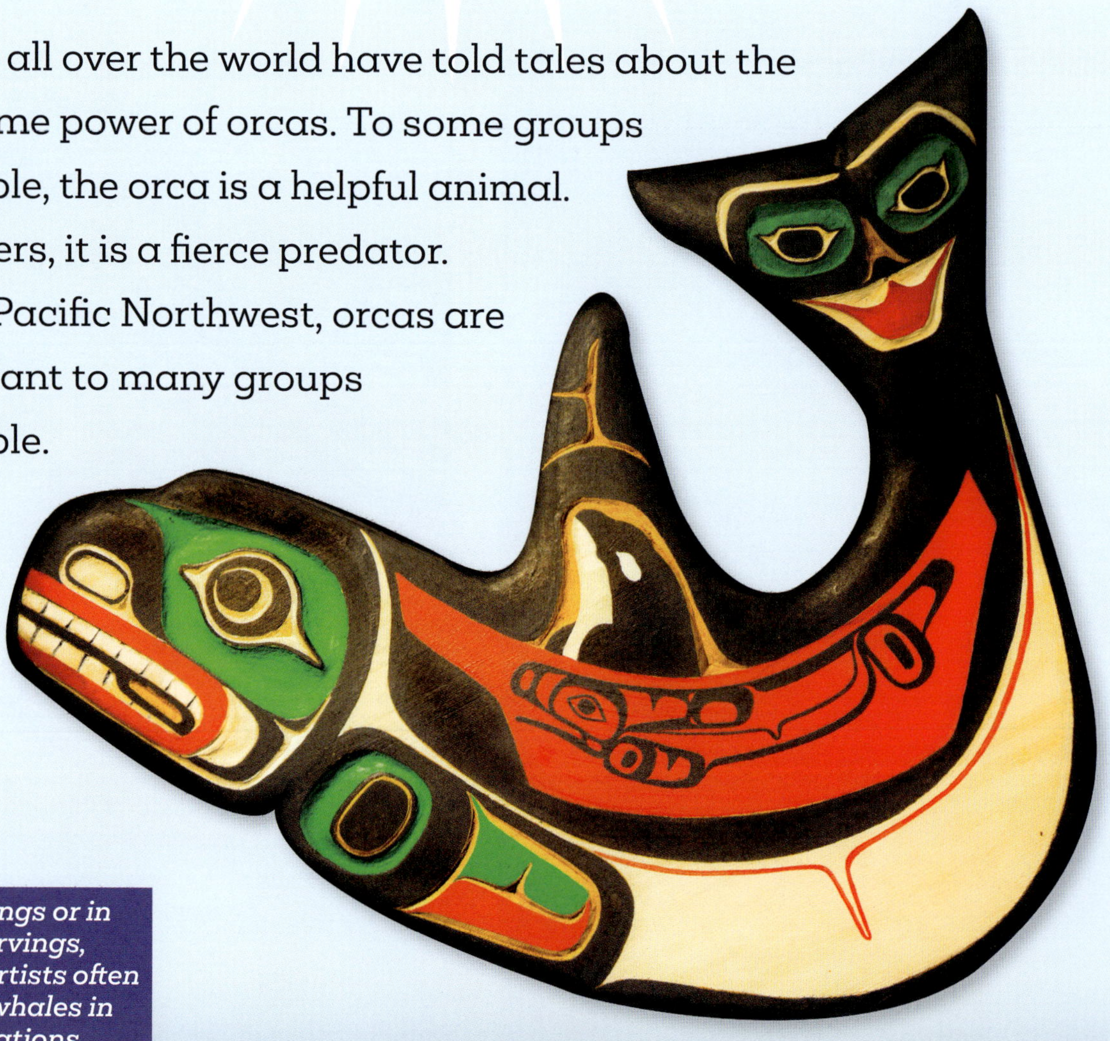

In paintings or in wood carvings, Tlingit artists often include whales in their creations.

The Haida (HI-dah) people viewed orcas as members of a group of powerful beings who live in the ocean.

Tlingit people tell a story about how a man carved the first orca from a piece of wood. In Tlingit beliefs, orcas are the protectors of the ocean.

A carved orca statue stands in front of a Haida building.

The very first people who lived in Japan, the Ainu (EYE-new), believed the orca was the master of the sea. Every year, the orca sent his friends, the salmon, up streams to visit the Ainu and the human world. Some of the salmon allowed themselves to be eaten by people. Other salmon swam back to report to the mighty orcas on how well the humans had welcomed them.

This man shows off traditional Ainu clothing.

ORCAS ON ICE

As part of their team logo, the Vancouver Canucks hockey team wears an orca in the shape of a C. One of the reasons is that many orcas live off the coast of Vancouver, Canada.

Here is one artist's idea of what Akhlut might look like.

People in other parts of the world tell stories about orcas, too. Most of these places are near the coastlines where orcas live. Inuit people in Alaska tell tales of Akhlut, an orca that could turn into a wolf and walk on land.

Orcas have also been movie stars. The most famous was Keiko, who starred in the 1997 movie *Free Willy*. In this family-friendly movie, a boy who lost his mother makes friends with an orca at an amusement park. The animal also lost his family when he was captured, so he and the boy have something in common.

Keiko was first moved to this larger tank.

When the animal's life is threatened, the boy saves him by helping him escape to the ocean. In real life, Keiko was living in a Mexican **marine park** in a tank that was too small. After he became a movie star, many people worked together to help him return to the wild ocean. Keiko did return to the ocean, but, sadly, died soon after.

After he was in the ocean, scientists were able to track Keiko.

That's not water. That is air vapor coming out as the orca surfaces to breathe.

Movies are cool, but the best place to see orcas is in the ocean. You might be lucky enough to live someplace where orcas swim near shore. Or maybe you'll see them when you're on vacation. Boat rides take visitors to places where they can see orcas swimming free.

If you're a seal, orcas are fierce and deadly enemies. If you're a human, however, orcas are amazing creatures to learn about. Few animals combine speed, size, and intelligence the way orcas do.

Whale-watching boats help people get a close look at these wonderful marine mammals.

GLOSSARY

acrobats (AK-roh-batz) people or animals that are good at gymnastics moves such as jumps and flips

dorsal (DOR-sul) on or near the back, such as a dorsal fin

echolocation (ek-oh-loh-KAY-shun) he ability to use sounds and their echoes to find your way or find food

kelp (KELP) a kind of seaweed that grows in long, thick strings and can form a dense underwater "forest"

mammals (MAMM-mulz) warm-blooded animals that breathe air, give birth to live babies, and feed them milk from their bodies

marine park (muh-REEN PARK) a special kind of zoo that has animals that live in the ocean

organ (OR-gun) a part of the body that is not bone or muscle and that has a special job

pods (PODZ) groups of orcas that live together like a family

predators (PRED-ih-turz) animals that eat other animals

prey (PRAY) an animal that is food for other animals

stunning (STUN-ning) making an animal unable to move, such as by hitting it hard

THINK ABOUT IT

Should orcas be kept in marine parks or aquariums? Why or why not?

What other sea animals remind you of orcas? Explain your answer.

Orcas used to be called killer whales. Do you think changing the animal's name has changed the way people feel about them?

FIND OUT MORE

IN THE LIBRARY

Rathburn, Betsy. *Orcas*. Minneapolis, MN: Bellwether, 2022.

Rose, Rachel. *Orca*. Minneapolis, MN: Bearport, 2021.

Scuh, Mari. *Orcas*. Minneapolis, MN: Jump! Inc., 2022.

ON THE WEB

Visit our website for links about orcas:
childsworld.com/links

Note to Parents, Teachers, and Librarians: We routinely verify our Web links to make sure they are safe and active sites. So encourage your readers to check them out!

INDEX

ABOUT THE AUTHOR

BETH ADELMAN writes and edits books about animals. She has won several awards from the Cat Writers Association and the Dog Writers Association of America, and served on the board of directors of the International Association of Animal Behavior Consultants. One of her favorite travel activities is visiting aquariums and zoos around the world. She has also been lucky enough to see wild orcas in Alaska.